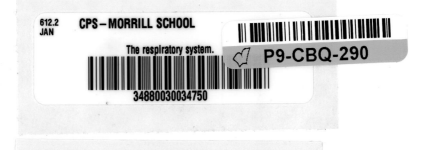
612.2
JAN

Jango-Cohen, Judith.

The respiratory
system.

34880030034750

$25.26

DATE		

THE RESPIRATORY SYSTEM

BY JUDITH JANGO-COHEN

𝄢 LERNER PUBLICATIONS COMPANY • MINNEAPOLIS

To Brad Cohen—may you always breathe easy, especially during the law boards

Many thanks to Joelle Riley, editor, for her discerning eye and her expertise

The photographs in this book are used with the permission of: © Royalty-Free/CORBIS, pp. 5, 8, 9, 10, 11, 20, 25, 34, 37; © Stock Image/SuperStock, p. 6; © Norbert Schaefer/CORBIS, p. 7; © Dwight R. Kuhn, pp. 12, 16, 40, 42, 43; © Baumgartner Olivia/CORBIS SYGMA, p. 13; © Diane M. Meyer, pp. 14, 47; © Todd Strand/Independent Picture Service, pp. 17, 31; © Gregg Otto/Visuals Unlimited, p.18; © Charles Gupton/CORBIS, p. 21; © David M. Martin, M.D./Photo Researchers, Inc., p. 22; © Gruppo05/SuperStock, p. 24; © CNRI/Photo Researchers, Inc., p. 26; © Innerspace Imaging/Photo Researchers, Inc., p. 28; © Gladden Willis, M.D./Visuals Unlimited, p. 29; © Eye of Science/Photo Researchers, Inc., p. 30; © Dr. David M. Phillips/Visuals Unlimited, pp. 32, 41, 48; © Photodisc Royalty Free by Getty Images, p. 36; © Lester V. Bergman/CORBIS, p. 38; © Catherine de Torquat/SuperStock, p. 46.

Cover photograph © BSIP Agency/Index Stock Imagery.

Illustrations on pp. 4, 15, 19, 23, 27, 33, 35, 39 by Laura Westlund, copyright © 2005 by Lerner Publications Company.

Copyright © 2005 by Judith Jango-Cohen

Lerner Publications Company
A division of Lerner Publishing Group
241 First Avenue North
Minneapolis, MN 55401 U.S.A

Website address: www.lernerbooks.com

Library of Congress Cataloging-in-Publication Data

Jango-Cohen, Judith.
   The respiratory system / by Judith Jango-Cohen.
     p.   cm. — (Early bird body systems)
   Includes index.
   Summary: Describes the respiratory system and how it works.
   ISBN: 0–8225–1250–5 (lib. bdg. : alk. paper)
   1. Respiratory organs—Juvenile literature. 2. Respiration—Juvenile literature.
[1. Respiratory system.] I. Title. II. Series.
QP121.J36 2005
612.2—dc22   2003023027

Manufactured in the United States of America
1 2 3 4 5 6 – JR – 10 09 08 07 06 05

CONTENTS

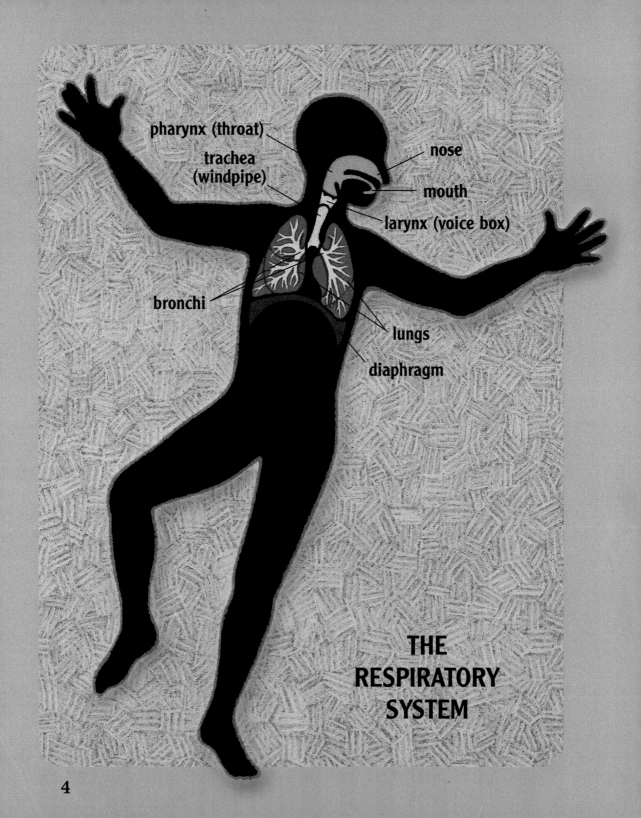

pharynx (throat)

trachea
(windpipe)

nose

mouth

larynx (voice box)

bronchi

lungs

diaphragm

**THE
RESPIRATORY
SYSTEM**

BE A WORD DETECTIVE

Can you find these words as you read about the respiratory system? Be a detective and try to figure out what they mean. You can turn to the glossary on page 46 for help.

alveoli	cilia	pharynx
bronchi	diaphragm	ribs
bronchioles	larynx	trachea
capillaries	lungs	vocal cords
carbon dioxide	mucus	
cells	oxygen	

CHAPTER 1

THE NEED TO BREATHE

You breathe slowly when you are asleep. How do you breathe when you run fast?

Imagine that you are sleeping. Your chest floats up and down. Quietly, your breath flows in and out.

Next, imagine that you are running a race. Your mouth sucks in air. Your nostrils stretch wide. At the finish line, you drop onto the grass. As you gasp for breath, your chest pumps up and down.

You breathe faster when you run than when you rest.

Have you ever wondered why your breathing changes? When you are relaxed, you take slow, shallow breaths. When you are active, you gulp fast, deep breaths. The more energy you use, the more air you need. But what does breathing have to do with energy?

Energy comes from food. When you eat food, you put energy into your body.

You need energy to run.
But you also need
energy to think.

Energy is locked up inside the food you eat.
The air you breathe lets this energy out. Air is
made of different gases. The gas that lets the
energy out of food is called oxygen (AHK-sih-jehn).

You always need to breathe because you
are always using energy. Even when you are
asleep, your heart is beating and your brain is
working. How much oxygen you need depends
upon how much energy you use.

After you run hard, you have to catch your breath. Your body needs more oxygen. It also has to get rid of lots of carbon dioxide.

When you breathe in, oxygen enters your body. Food is in your body too. Oxygen combines with the food. Then energy is given off. A gas called carbon dioxide (dy-AHK-side) is also given off. Carbon dioxide is harmful. You must quickly get rid of it. The carbon dioxide goes into your lungs so you can breathe it out.

The more active you are, the faster you breathe. You take in more oxygen and give off more carbon dioxide.

Your body has many different systems to help you breathe, move, and digest your food. These systems all work together so you can do things like play basketball.

Many parts of your body help you to breathe. These body parts are called the respiratory (REHS-puh-ruh-tor-ee) system. Most of the time, you are not thinking about breathing. But your respiratory system still works. You may be in school running a race. Or you may be in bed dreaming about winning one.

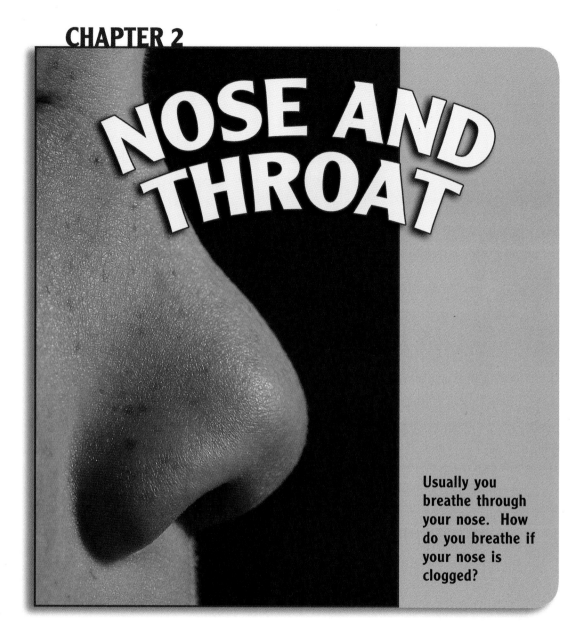

CHAPTER 2

NOSE AND THROAT

Usually you breathe through your nose. How do you breathe if your nose is clogged?

Your nose is like the door to your respiratory system. Most of the air that you breathe goes in through your nose.

Blowing your nose helps to unclog it. Then you can breathe more easily.

But what happens when you have a cold and your nose gets clogged? Then you have to breathe through your mouth. Your mouth is like an emergency entrance. You use it when your nose is blocked or when you need extra air.

Breathing through your nose is healthier than breathing through your mouth. Your nose cleans dust and germs out of the air you breathe. Hairs in your nose snag dust. Dust also gets stuck in mucus (MYOO-kuhs). Mucus is a slimy liquid that coats the inside of your nose. Germs are too small for the hairs to catch. But they stick to the mucus. Germs trapped in your nose do not enter your body to make you sick.

If you breathe in too much dust, you may have to sneeze! Sneezing blows dust out of your nose.

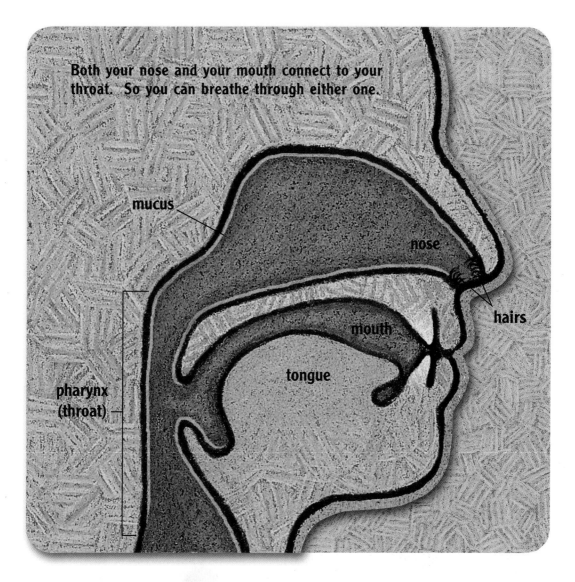

Both your nose and your mouth connect to your throat. So you can breathe through either one.

mucus

nose

hairs

mouth

tongue

pharynx (throat)

Mucus does more than trap dirt and germs. Mucus is wet. So mucus moistens the air you breathe. Air breathed in through your nose does not dry out your throat.

15

When you play outside in the winter, your nose warms the air you breathe. This way, freezing air does not enter your throat and lungs.

Besides cleaning and moistening the air, your nose also heats it. Your nose is warm. Air is heated as it flows through your nose. Even frosty air is warmed. This keeps the air from chilling your body.

Cleaned, moistened, and warmed air goes from your nose into your throat. Another name for your throat is your pharynx (FAR-ihngks).

Air breathed in through your mouth enters the pharynx too. So do food and drink.

The lower part of the pharynx splits into two tubes. One tube connects to the stomach. This is where the food and liquids go. The other tube leads to the lungs. This is where the air goes. This tube for the air is called the larynx (LAR-ihngks).

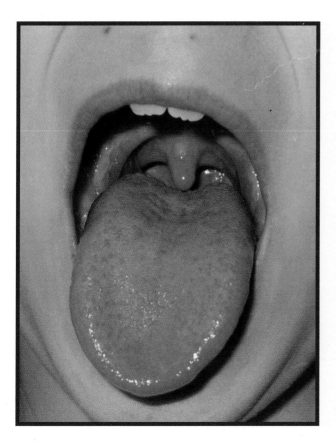

Your pharynx is behind your mouth.

CHAPTER 3

THE LARYNX

You use your pharynx for both eating and breathing. Can you swallow and breathe at the same time?

Both food and air travel down your pharynx. But then they go in different directions. Food moves down to your stomach. Air enters your larynx and heads for your lungs. Have you ever wondered how this happens without a mix-up?

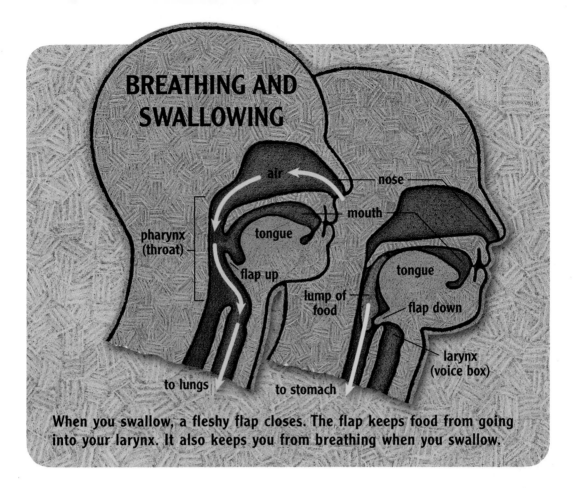

BREATHING AND SWALLOWING

nose

mouth

air

pharynx
(throat)

tongue

flap up

tongue

lump of
food

flap down

larynx
(voice box)

to lungs

to stomach

When you swallow, a fleshy flap closes. The flap keeps food from going into your larynx. It also keeps you from breathing when you swallow.

Try to swallow and breathe at the same time. You cannot do it! When you swallow, a flap closes over your larynx. It fits like the lid on a box. The flap keeps you from breathing. Put your fingers on your neck while you swallow slowly. You can feel your larynx press up against your tongue while the flap closes.

Since your larynx is covered when you swallow, food cannot go into it. Food heads safely down the tube to your stomach.

When the flap covers your larynx, you can drink without choking.

Talking with food in your mouth is dangerous. Food may go down the wrong way, causing you to choke.

But when you talk or laugh, your larynx is not covered. If you talk while eating, food may accidentally fall into your larynx. This blocks your larynx and makes you choke. Right away you start to cough. Coughing sends bursts of air upward through your larynx. The air knocks the food out. Once your larynx is unblocked, you can breathe again.

Air flowing through your larynx passes between two stretchy bands called vocal cords. When you breathe, your vocal cords lie loosely against the sides of your larynx.

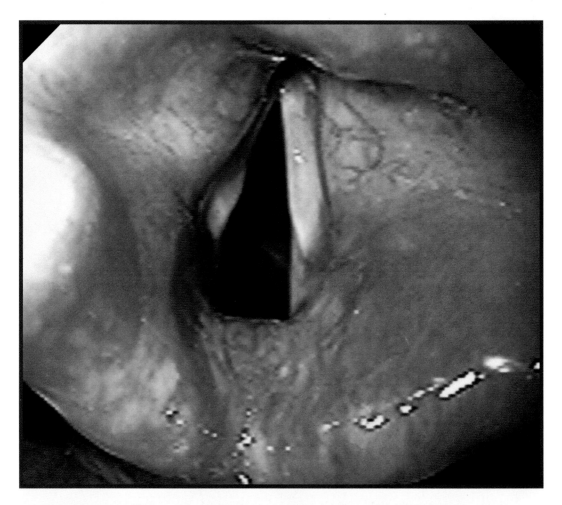

This picture shows a person's larynx and vocal cords. The space between your vocal cords lets air pass through so you can breathe.

HOW YOU SPEAK

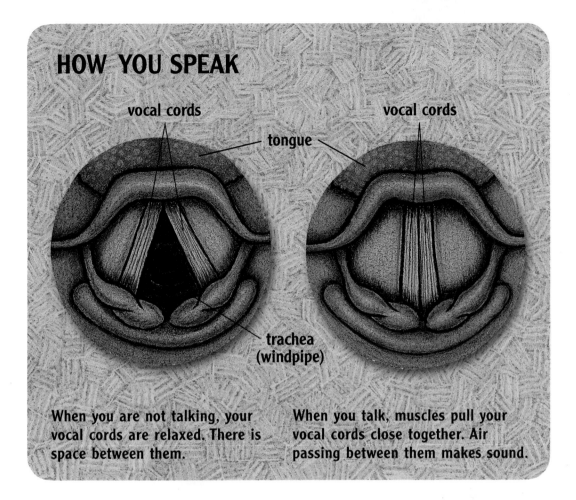

vocal cords   vocal cords

tongue

trachea
(windpipe)

When you are not talking, your vocal cords are relaxed. There is space between them.

When you talk, muscles pull your vocal cords close together. Air passing between them makes sound.

When you speak, muscles pull your vocal cords together. This leaves only a small slit between them. Air moving through the slit makes the vocal cords vibrate, or shake. To feel your vocal cords vibrating, place your fingers on your neck. Then talk, hum, or sing.

When your vocal cords vibrate, they make sounds. The tighter the vocal cords are stretched, the higher the sound is. You can see how this works. Pluck a rubber band as you stretch it tighter and tighter. Listen to how the sound changes.

A guitar's strings are attached to pegs. The pegs can be turned to make the strings tighter or looser. Then the sound the strings make becomes higher or lower. Vocal cords work in a similar way.

You can sing high and low notes by tightening and loosening your vocal cords.

Small vocal cords make higher sounds than big vocal cords. Children have smaller vocal cords than adults have. So children have higher voices than adults. As you grow, your vocal cords get bigger. And your voice becomes lower.

CHAPTER 4

FROM LARYNX TO LUNGS

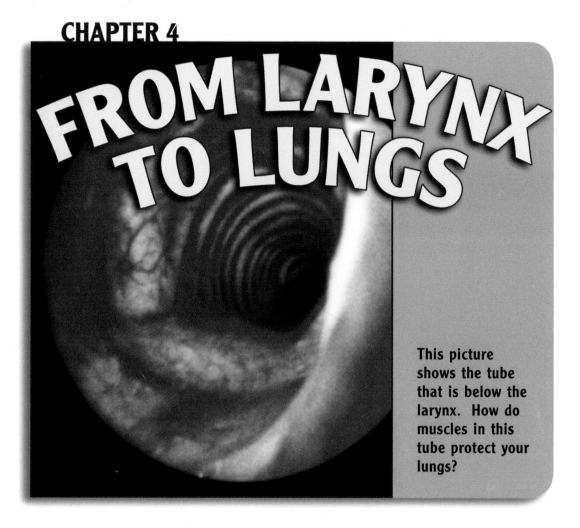

This picture shows the tube that is below the larynx. How do muscles in this tube protect your lungs?

Your larynx is connected to a tube called the trachea (TRAY-kee-uh). Muscles and stiff bands line the walls of the trachea. If food falls through your larynx and into your trachea, the muscles of the trachea tighten around it. This stops the food from going down into your lungs.

26

THE RESPIRATORY SYSTEM

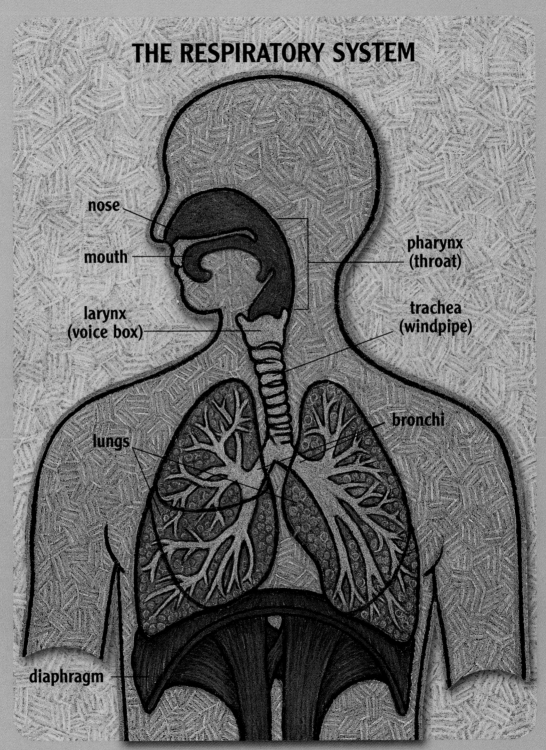

nose

mouth

pharynx
(throat)

larynx
(voice box)

trachea
(windpipe)

bronchi

lungs

diaphragm

The bottom part of your trachea divides into two branches. One branch goes to the right lung. The other branch goes to the left lung. These tubes that go to your lungs are called bronchi (BRAHNG-kye).

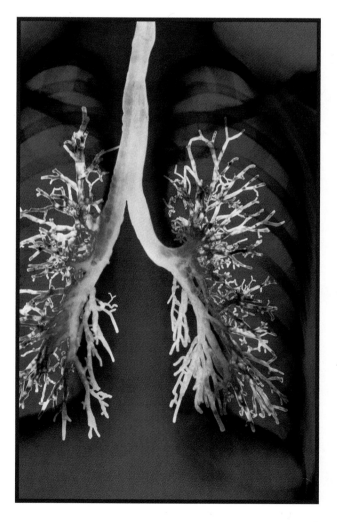

This is an X-ray picture of the tubes inside a person's lungs. The big tube at the top is the trachea. The two thick branches are the bronchi.

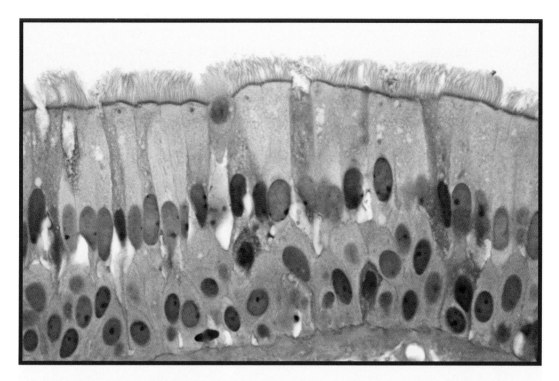

The walls of the bronchi are made of different kinds of cells. Some of the cells make mucus.

Your bronchi make mucus. The mucus traps dirt and germs that were not caught by the mucus in your nose. That way, they do not go into your lungs. But the bronchi must get rid of the dirty mucus. Otherwise, more and more mucus would build up. The bronchi would get clogged. You would not be able to breathe.

Tiny hairs in the bronchi get rid of the dirty mucus. The hairs are called cilia (SIHL-ee-uh). The cilia wave back and forth like paddles. Cilia push the mucus up and away from your lungs. When the mucus reaches your pharynx, you can cough it out. You can also swallow it. Chemicals in your stomach destroy the germs trapped in the mucus.

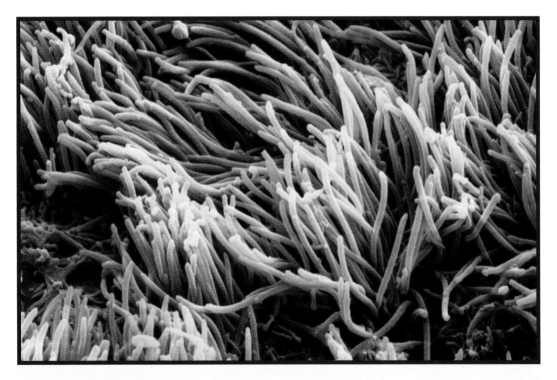

Cilia look like tiny, waving hairs.

Always cover your mouth when you cough. This stops germs in the mucus from going into the air. Then be sure to wash your hands.

Air has traveled from nose or mouth to pharynx, larynx, trachea, and bronchi. It has been cleaned, moistened, and warmed. It is ready to be delivered to your lungs.

CHAPTER 5

THE LUNGS

The inside of a lung looks sort of like a sponge. What protects the soft lungs from being hurt?

Inside your lungs, the bronchi divide into smaller and smaller tubes. The tiniest of these tubes are called bronchioles (BRAHNG-kee-ohlz). Bronchioles are a bit smaller across than the millimeter spaces on your ruler. Each bronchiole connects to a bundle of alveoli (al-VEE-uh-lye). Alveoli look like tiny balloons. Millions of bronchioles and alveoli are packed together in your lungs.

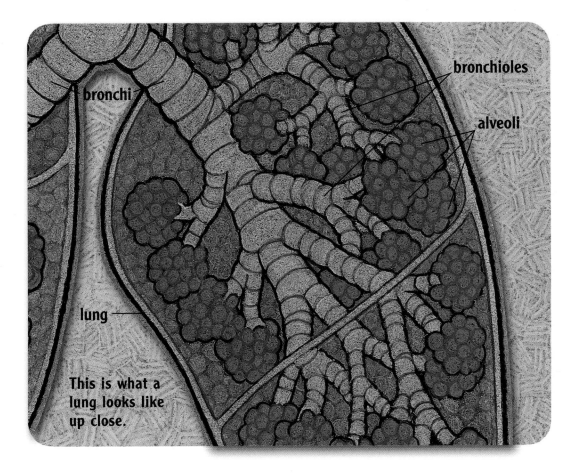

bronchi

bronchioles

alveoli

lung

This is what a lung looks like up close.

You cannot feel your lungs when you touch the center of your chest. Instead, you feel the flat bone that protects them. Connected to this bone are your ribs. Your ribs surround your lungs like a cage. Behind your lungs, your ribs connect to your backbone. Your backbone also helps protect your lungs.

Your diaphragm helps you to take a big breath so you can blow out a candle.

Your chest also has many muscles. All these muscles move whenever you breathe. Below your lungs is a big, dome-shaped muscle called the diaphragm (DYE-uh-fram). The diaphragm separates your chest from your belly.

Take your deepest breath and hold it. Can you feel your diaphragm tighten? The diaphragm is pushing downward. This gives your lungs more room in your chest. Air rushes into this extra space when you breathe in.

Now let the air out slowly. When you breathe out, your diaphragm relaxes. When the diaphragm relaxes, it takes up more room. Your lungs are squeezed into a smaller space. The air is pushed out.

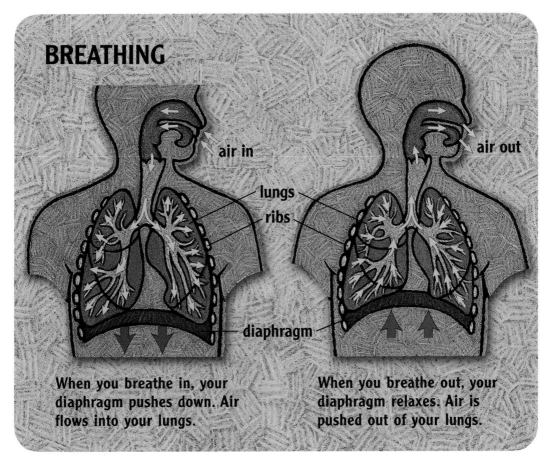

BREATHING

air in

lungs

ribs

air out

diaphragm

When you breathe in, your diaphragm pushes down. Air flows into your lungs.

When you breathe out, your diaphragm relaxes. Air is pushed out of your lungs.

Muscles between your ribs move along with your diaphragm. They lift your rib cage away from your lungs when you breathe in. This gives your lungs more room. Put your fingers on your ribs as you take a breath. Notice that your ribs move outward and up. When you breathe out, your ribs move down and in.

When you take a deep breath, your ribs move up and out. This makes room for more air in your lungs.

Doctors listen to your lungs to make sure they are working well.

Your lungs are oxygen's last stop in your respiratory system. From your lungs, oxygen travels to every part of your body.

CHAPTER 6

AROUND THE BODY

The alveoli in the lungs look like tiny balloons. How does oxygen get from the alveoli to the rest of the body?

Oxygen moves from your lungs to the rest of your body by entering your blood. Each of the alveoli in your lungs is surrounded by capillaries (KAP-uh-layr-eez). Capillaries are tiny blood vessels. When oxygen leaves the alveoli, it passes into the blood in the capillaries. The blood carries the oxygen to your heart. Your heart pumps the oxygen-filled blood around your body.

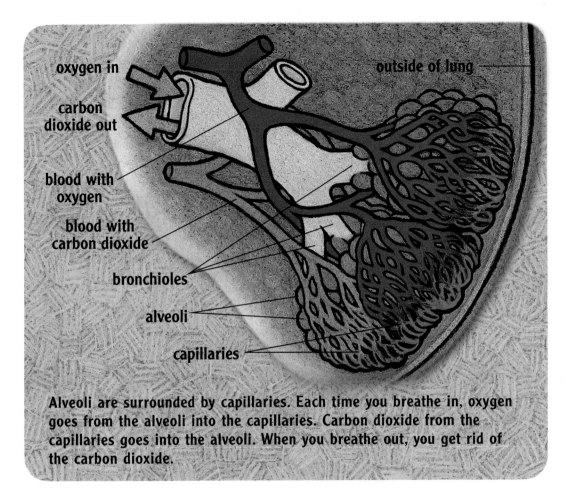

oxygen in

carbon dioxide out

blood with oxygen

blood with carbon dioxide

bronchioles

alveoli

capillaries

outside of lung

Alveoli are surrounded by capillaries. Each time you breathe in, oxygen goes from the alveoli into the capillaries. Carbon dioxide from the capillaries goes into the alveoli. When you breathe out, you get rid of the carbon dioxide.

Then the oxygen leaves the blood. It enters all the cells of your body. In the cells, oxygen combines with food to release energy. But carbon dioxide gas is also released. It passes out of the cells and into the capillaries. Flowing blood carries the carbon dioxide away.

The blood and carbon dioxide soon reach your heart. The heart pumps them to the capillaries in your lungs. In your lungs, carbon dioxide passes out of the capillaries and into the alveoli. When you breathe out, carbon dioxide leaves the alveoli. It travels into the bronchioles, the bronchi, the trachea, the larynx, and the pharynx. Then it goes out through your nose or mouth.

When you breathe out, you get rid of carbon dioxide.

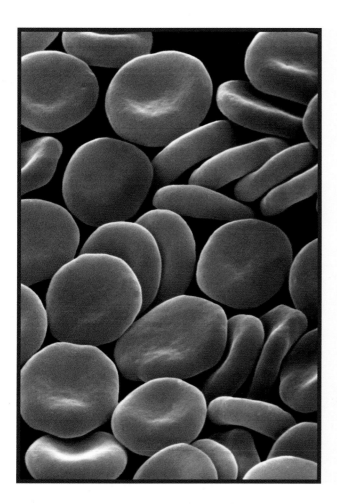

Blood has red blood cells and white blood cells. This picture shows red blood cells. Red blood cells carry oxygen through the body.

Your respiratory system never stops working. It brings in oxygen and gets rid of carbon dioxide. But your respiratory system does not work alone. It needs the help of your heart and blood vessels. They move oxygen and carbon dioxide swiftly around your body.

Without oxygen, you would not have the energy to move a muscle.

A lot is happening inside you. Muscles in your chest are tightening and relaxing. Gases are moving through tubes and alveoli and into your blood. Your heart is pushing blood through your body. You are using energy.

Were you thinking about all this? You probably thought you were just relaxing and reading a book!

Your respiratory system works on its own. If it didn't, you would have to think about breathing all the time!

ON SHARING A BOOK

When you share a book with a child, you show that reading is important. To get the most out of the experience, read in a comfortable, quiet place. Turn off the television and limit other distractions, such as telephone calls.

   Be prepared to start slowly. Take turns reading parts of this book. Stop occasionally and discuss what you're reading. Talk about the photographs. If the child begins to lose interest, stop reading. When you pick up the book again, revisit the parts you have already read.

BE A VOCABULARY DETECTIVE

The word list on page 5 contains words that are important in understanding the topic of this book. Be word detectives and search for the words as you read the book together. Talk about what the words mean and how they are used in the sentence. Do any of these words have more than one meaning? You will find the words defined in a glossary on page 46.

WHAT ABOUT QUESTIONS?

Use questions to make sure the child understands the information in this book. Here are some suggestions:

> What did this paragraph tell us? What does this picture show? What do you think we'll learn about next? What does the respiratory system do? Why do you breathe faster when you run? Why can't you breathe and swallow at the same time? Why do adults have lower voices than children have? What is your favorite part of the book? Why?

If the child has questions, don't hesitate to respond with questions of your own, such as What do *you* think? Why? What is it that you don't know? If the child can't remember certain facts, turn to the index.

INTRODUCING THE INDEX

The index helps readers find information without searching through the whole book. Turn to the index on page 48. Choose an entry such as *nose* and ask the child to use the index to find out why it is better to breathe through the nose than the mouth. Repeat with as many entries as you like. Ask the child to point out the differences between an index and a glossary. (The index helps readers find information, while the glossary tells readers what words mean.)

LEARN MORE ABOUT
THE RESPIRATORY SYSTEM

BOOKS
Furgang, Kathy. *My Lungs.* New York: PowerKids Press, 2001. Follow oxygen and carbon dioxide through your body. Photos of 3-D models help to explain how the respiratory system works.

LeVert, Suzanne. *The Lungs.* New York: Benchmark Books, 2002. This book describes the respiratory system and lung illnesses such as colds and asthma.

Royston, Angela. *Why Do I Sneeze? And Other Questions about Breathing.* Chicago: Heinemann Library, 2003. Find out what hiccups are, what happens when you breathe polluted air, and more.

Stille, Darlene R. *The Respiratory System.* New York: Children's Press, 1997. This book describes how the parts of the respiratory system work.

WEBSITES
Inside the Human Body: The Respiratory System
<http://www.lung.ca/children/index_kids.html>
This website has lots of information, plus activities and games.

My Body
<http://www.kidshealth.org/kid/body/mybody.html>
This fun website has information on body systems, plus movies, games, and activities.

Pathfinders for Kids: The Respiratory System—The Air Bags
<http://infozone.imcpl.org/kids_resp.htm>
This is a list of resources you can use to learn more about the respiratory system.

Your Gross and Cool Body: Respiratory System
<http://yucky.kids.discovery.com/flash/body/pg000138.html>
This site has information about the respiratory system and other body systems, with a special focus on gross body sounds and yucky body parts.

GLOSSARY

alveoli (al-VEE-uh-lye): tiny, air-filled pouches in the lungs

bronchi (BRAHNG-kye): the two tubes that connect the windpipe to the lungs

bronchioles (BRAHNG-kee-ohlz): tiny tubes inside the lungs

capillaries (KAP-uh-layr-eez): tiny blood vessels. Capillaries surround each of the alveoli in the lungs.

carbon dioxide (dy-AHK-side): the gas that is made when oxygen combines with food

cells: the building blocks of living things

cilia (SIHL-ee-uh): tiny hairs in the air passages. Cilia wave back and forth like paddles to push mucus toward the throat.

diaphragm (DYE-uh-fram): the dome-shaped muscle below the lungs that is used in breathing

larynx (LAR-ihngks): the voice box. A flap closes over the larynx when you swallow.

lungs: spongy sacks in the chest that put oxygen into the blood and take carbon dioxide out of it

mucus (MYOO-kuhs): a thick, sticky liquid that traps germs and dirt in the air passages

oxygen (AHK-sih-jehn): the gas that combines with food to release energy

pharynx (FAR-ihngks): the throat. Passages from the nose and mouth connect to the pharynx.

ribs: bones that surround the lungs like a cage

trachea (TRAY-kee-uh): the windpipe. The trachea connects the larynx to the bronchi.

vocal cords: two stretchy bands inside the voice box that vibrate and make voice sounds

INDEX

Pages listed in **bold** type refer to photographs.

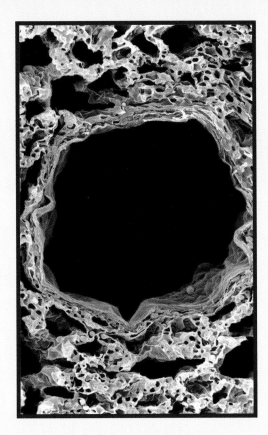